MW01098191

GALE

CENGAGE Learning

Novels for Students, Volume 4 Copyright Notice

Gale Research
27500 Drake Rd.
Farmington Hills, MI 48331-3535

ISBN 0-7876-2115-3
ISSN 1094-3552

Printed in the United States of America.
10 9 8 7 6 5 4 3

Les Misérables

Victor Hugo

1862

Introduction

When Victor Hugo's novel *Les Misérables* first
came out in 1862, people in Paris and elsewhere
lined up to buy it. Although critics were less
receptive, the novel was an instant popular success.
The French word "misérables" means both poor
wretches and scoundrels or villains. The novel
offers a huge cast that includes both kinds of
"misérables." A product of France's most prominent
Romantic writer, *Les Misérables* ranges far and
wide. It paints a vivid picture of Paris's seamier
side, discusses the causes and results of revolution,

and includes discourses on topics ranging from the Battle of Waterloo to Parisian street slang. But the two central themes that dominate the novel are the moral redemption of its main character, Jean Valjean, an ex-convict, and the moral redemption of a nation through revolution. Victor Hugo said: "I condemn slavery, I banish poverty, I teach ignorance, I treat disease, I lighten the night, and I hate hatred. That is what I am, and that is why I have written *Les Misérables.*" The novel is a critical statement against human suffering, poverty, and ignorance. Its purpose is as much political as it is artistic.

Author Biography

As a novelist, poet, political activist, and painter, Victor Hugo was a central figure in the Romantic movement of nineteenth-century France. Both his family and his times influenced Hugo's social views and politics, which included a deep concern with human rights, social injustice, and poverty as the root of evil. Born in Besançon, France, in 1802, Hugo grew up in the years of Napoleon Bonaparte's empire. In 1815, the empire collapsed at the Battle of Waterloo, which Hugo describes in detail in *Les Misérables,* and a constitutional monarchy was established. His father was a general in the Napoleonic army with republican sympathies while his middle-class mother had royalist leanings. The young Hugo spent a large part of his childhood in Paris with his mother. He also traveled through Europe in his father's wake and glimpsed the Napoleonic campaigns. After attending school in Paris, he married his childhood love, Adèle Foucher, in 1822.

In that same year, Hugo published his first volume of poetry, beginning a long and diverse literary career that also included drama and novels. He was acquainted with many major figures on the intellectual and artistic scene. His political convictions changed over time as various French governments rose and fell, but his belief in human rights was consistent. In a letter to a friend describing why he wrote *Les Misérables,* Hugo said: "If the radical is the ideal, yes, I am a radical. ... A society which admits poverty, a religion which admits hell, a humanity which sanctions war, seem to me an inferior society, an inferior religion and humanity, and it is towards the higher society, the higher humanity and religion that I turn: society without a king, humanity without frontiers, religion without a book.... I condemn slavery, I banish poverty, I teach ignorance, I treat disease, I lighten the night, and I hate hatred. That is what I am, and that is why I have written *Les Misérables.*"

The 1840s to the 1860s were an active time for the writer. He was elected to the Académie Française in 1841 and to the peerage in 1845 in recognition of his literary achievements. The late 1840s marked a period of serious political involvement for Hugo. He spoke up in the Chamber of Peers, criticizing the legal system and the treatment of the poor, themes to which he returned in *Les Misérables.* Disillusioned with monarchism, he publicly espoused republicanism and participated in the revolution of 1848. These experiences gave him firsthand knowledge of what barricade fighting was like, which he used in the novel. Louis Napoleon, the elected president of the newly established republic, seized power in a coup d'état in 1851. Hugo criticized the new ruler and ended up in exile, first in Belgium, then later on the Isle of Guernsey in the English Channel, where he remained until 1870. It was during this exile that he wrote most of *Les Misérables.*

Les Misérables was first published in 1862,

appearing simultaneously in cities across Europe. In spite of a mixed critical reaction, the novel, with its championing of the poor and disenfranchised, was an immediate popular success in France and abroad. It sealed Hugo's reputation as a legend.

Upon his return to France in 1870, he received a hero's welcome. He continued to write for the rest of his life, but abstained from politics. After his death in 1885, Victor Hugo lay in state under the Arc de Triomphe and was buried in the Pantheon, in the heart of his beloved city, Paris.

Plot Summary

Les Misérables is the story of four people, Bishop Myriel, Jean Valjean, Fantine, and Marius Pontmercy, who meet, part, then meet again during the most agitated decades of nineteenth-century France. It also tells the story of the 1832 revolution and describes the unpleasant side of Paris. The novel is in essence a plea for humane treatment of the poor and for equality among all citizens.

Part I—Fantine

The year is 1815 and Napoleon has just been defeated at Waterloo. Bishop Myriel lives a quiet life as a just man, who is especially sympathetic toward the poor, bandits, and convicts. One day a strange man asks for shelter at his home and, with his usual compassion, the bishop gives him room and board. This man is Jean Valjean, who has just been released from prison after serving a lengthy, unjust sentence, during which he tried to escape numerous times. Valjean is angry, hurt, and vengeful. His soul has "withered" and all but died. The bishop urges him to replace anger with goodwill in order to be worthy of respect: "You have left a place of suffering. But listen, there will be more joy in heaven over the tears of a repentant sinner, than over the white robes of a hundred good men. If you are leaving that sorrowful place with hate and anger against men, you are worthy of compassion; if you leave it with goodwill, gentleness, and peace, you are better than any of us."

Valjean listens. Nevertheless, he decides to rob the good bishop. During the night, he runs away with the bishop's silver. He is caught and brought back to the bishop, who tells the police that he himself gave Valjean these precious objects. Later Bishop Myriel tells Valjean, "you belong no longer to evil, but to good. It is your soul I am buying for you. I withdraw it from dark thoughts and from the spirit of perdition and I give it to God!" Valjean is stunned. After he steals a coin from a little boy, he has an epiphany: "he could see his life, and it seemed horrible; his soul, and it seemed frightful. There was, however, a gentler light shining on that life and soul."

Fantine is a seamstress unjustly fired once her employer learns about her scandalous past. Abandoned by her lover, she is hungry, destitute, and unable to care for her daughter, Cosette. First she sells her hair, then her teeth, before finally prostituting herself. At this stage of the story, Fantine has "endured all, borne all, experienced all, suffered all, lost all, wept for all. She is resigned, with that resignation that resembles indifference as death resembles sleep." She leaves two-year-old Cosette to the care of the Thénardiers, who run a tavern in the outskirts of Paris. Cosette is poorly treated by the couple and their two daughters. The Thénardiers view Cosette as their domestic slave, all the while demanding more and more money for

Cosette's care. Fantine must continue selling her body to pay for Cosette's keep.

Valjean assumes a new identity as Monsieur Madeleine, and becomes a good citizen, a rich industrialist, and ultimately mayor. Valjean saves Fantine from the police (headed by Inspector Javert) once he discovers she was fired from the very factory under his care. He wants to redeem her, but it is too late. Fantine is sick and soon dies.

At the same time, Champmathieu is falsely accused of being Valjean by Inspector Javert, whose lifelong goal has been to find the escaped convict Valjean. Javert was a "formidable man" whose mother was a fortune-teller and whose father was in the galleys. "His stare was cold and as piercing as a gimlet. His whole life was contained in these two words: waking and watching." After a long night of hesitation—to accuse Champmathieu would save him from Javert, to keep silent would send an innocent man to death—Valjean decides to confess his true identity to save the wrongly accused man:

> He declared that his life, in truth, did have an object. But what object? to conceal his name? to deceive the police? was it for so petty a thing that he had done all that he had done? had he no other object, which was the great one, which was the true one? To save, not his body, but his soul. To become honest and good again. To be an upright man! was it not that, above all, that alone, which

he had always wished, and which the bishop had enjoined upon him!... To deliver himself up, to save this man stricken by so ghastly a mistake, to reassume his name, to become again from duty the convict Jean Valjean; that was really to achieve his resurrection, and to close for ever the hell from whence he had emerged! to fall into it in appearance, was to emerge in reality! he must do that! all he had done was nothing, if he did not do that! all his life was useless, all his suffering was lost. He had only to ask the question: "What is the use?"

When the unyielding Javert arrests him, Valjean escapes, and a long hunt begins.

Part II—Cosette

Valjean does not run far. Fantine has told him about Cosette, so he goes to the Thénardiers' and saves the little girl from her terrible life. They settle in Paris, where they constantly have to hide from Javert's eye. They finally find shelter in a convent, the Petit-Picpus, where they spend five happy years of redemption: "Everything around him, this quiet garden, these balmy flowers, these children, shouting with joy, these meek and simple women, this silent cloister, gradually entered into all his being, and his soul subsided into silence.... His whole heart melted in gratitude and he loved more and more."

Part III—Marius

Marius is a young student, and like many other young men of his generation, he is passionately interested in Napoleon: "Napoleon had become to him the people-man as Jesus was the God-man." In Paris he meets a group a young radical students, the Friends of the ABC, who are very much like him and who convert him to republicanism: "my mother is the republic." One day, he spots in a park a young girl, wallking with her father. "She was a marvelous beauty. The only remark which could be made … is that the contradiction between her look, which was sad, and her smile, which was joyous, gave to her countenance something a little wild." He sees her again the next day, and the next, until, six months later, he falls in love with her. It is the fifteen-year-old Cosette.

Part IV—Saint Denis

Cosette has noticed Marius and falls in love with him, but she does not want Valjean to know about it. One day Marius writes to her and they secretly meet: "these two hearts poured themselves into each other, so that at the end of an hour, it was the young man who had the young girl's soul and the young girl who had the soul of the young man." Valjean suspects nothing until he accidentally intercepts one of Marius's letters.

Part V—Jean Valjean

Workers and republican students are on the barricades, opposing the police and the army of the monarchy. Many of the revolutionaries are killed in the struggle. Valjean discovers Marius and Cosette's love, but still saves Marius's life on the barricades. He carries the wounded and unconscious young man through the Paris sewers. He has one last confrontation with Javert, his old nemesis, who is at his mercy. He decides to let him go. Moved by this gesture and appalled at himself, Javert kills himself: "Terrible situation! to be moved! To be granite, and to doubt! to be ice and to melt! to feel your fingers suddenly open! to lose your hold, appalling thing!... The projectile man no longer knowing his road, and recoiling!" Still, many died, including Gavroche, a little Parisian boy whose courage inspired the fighters of the barricades.

Cosette restores Marius to health, and they decide to get married. On the wedding day, Marius meets Valjean, who tells him who he really is, a convict still hunted by the police, and that Cosette does not know anything about his unsavory past. However, Valjean does not tell Marius that he saved his life during the insurrections. Marius wants to help him win his pardon, but Valjean refuses: "I need pardon of none but one, that is my conscience." Marius decides to stay silent, but he is horrified by the revelations. Valjean stops visiting the young couple. Soon, Marius learns that he was saved by him and, accompanied by Cosette, rushes to Valjean's home, but it is too late: Valjean is dying. Uttering his last words, Valjean advises them, "There is scarcely anything else in the world but that: to love one another." He is buried under a blank stone.

Characters

Bahorel

Bahorel is a student and a member of the ABC Society, a secret revolutionary group of students and workers. But he has no respect for authority and is a real troublemaker, liking nothing better than a good fight.

Mademoiselle Baptistine

The unmarried sister of the Bishop of Digne, she lives with him and runs his household. She is a gentle, respectable woman who does good works.

Bishop of Digne

See Charles Myriel

Bossuet

A member of the ABC Society, Bossuet is a law student. He is cheerful but unlucky; everything he undertakes seems to go wrong.

Combeferre

Combeferre is a member of the ABC Society, a student, and a philosopher of revolution. He has a scientific mind and dreams of the inventions of the future and how they will benefit the human race.

Cosette

Cosette is the illegitimate daughter of Fantine, a Parisian "grisette" (working woman) whose lover, Félix Tholomyés, abandons her when she is pregnant. Valjean rescues Cosette from the Thénardiers, and she becomes the love of his life and the motivation for his goodness. She is raised and educated in a convent. When she and Valjean move out into the real Paris, she turns into a beautiful young Parisian woman and falls in love with Marius Pontmercy.

Courfeyrac

A member of the ABC Society, Courfeyrac becomes Marius's friend and takes him in.

Enjolras

Enjolras is a leader of the ABC Society. Marius first meets him there and ends up fighting with him on the barricade. The only son of rich parents, Enjolras is a student of the Revolution and has "a nature at once scholarly and warlike." He is indifferent to women and pleasure, but passionate about justice. Enjolras defines what he is fighting for in a speech on the barricade: "Citizens, no matter what happens today, in defeat no less than in victory, we shall be making a revolution. [...

Equality] means, in civic terms, an equal outlet for all talents; in political terms, that all votes will carry the same weight; and in religious terms that all beliefs will enjoy equal rights. Equality has a means at its disposal—compulsory free education. The right to learn the alphabet, that is where we must start."

Fantine

Fantine is a Parisian "grisette," or working woman, who falls in love with a student, Félix Tholomyés. Just after Félix breaks off their relationship, she gives birth to their daughter, Cosette. From that point forward her life is a downward spiral. She gives up her child to the mercenary Thénardiers and finds a job in her home town, but is dismissed when her supervisor finds out about her past. She struggles to make ends meet, selling everything she has: her hair, her teeth, and herself (becoming a prostitute). Fantine represents society's cruelty to the poor and its degradation of poor women in particular. Only Valjean shows her any kindness.

Media Adaptations

- Recorded in 1988, *Les Misérables* is available from Dove Books on Tape in an abridged version read by Christopher Cazenove.

- *Les Misérables* was adapted for the stage as a musical by Alain Boublil and Claude-Michel Schonberg, with the lyrics composed by Herbert Kretzmer. In 1995, the tenth anniversary concert in Royal Albert Hall, London, was released as a movie by Columbia Tristar Home Video. The musical is also available as a sound recording from Geffen produced in 1987. This version features the original Broadway cast.

- *Les Misérables* was made into a film in 1935, starring Fredric March,

Charles Laughton, Cedric Hardwicke, Rochelle Hudson, and John Beal. Directed by Richard Boleslawski, this adaptation is detailed and faithful to the novel, except for a changed ending. Considered a classic, the film received Academy Award nominations for Best Cinematography and Best Picture.

- There are many French film adaptations of the novel. A version released in 1957 stars Jean Gabin, Daniele Delorme, Bernard Blier, Bourvil, Gianni Esposito, and Serge Reggiani. Directed by Jean-Paul LeChanois, the film is in French with English subtitles.

- A version directed by Glenn Jordan was made for television in 1978, starring Richard Jordan, Anthony Perkins, John Gielgud, Cyril Cusack, Flora Robson, Celia Johnson, and Claude Dauphin.

- An animated version of *Les Misérables* appeared in 1979, produced by Toei Animation Company.

- A 1994 film version of the novel transferred its setting to early twentieth-century France. Directed, produced, and adapted by Claude

Lelouch, the movie, starring Jean-Paul Belmondo, Michel Boujenah, Alessandrea Martines, and Annie Girador, received a Golden Globe award for Best Foreign Film.

Pére Fauchelevent

When Fauchelevent, an elderly carrier, gets caught beneath the wheels of his own cart, Valjean rescues him and afterward finds work for him as a gardener in a Paris convent. In doing so, Valjean risks giving away his identity to Javert, who is already suspicious, by showing his great strength. But Fauchelevent repays Valjean by taking him and Cosette in when they are on the run from the police. Fauchelevent, an educated peasant, is both shrewd and good-willed. He recognizes his debt and finds the means to repay it.

Feuilly

A member of the ABC Society of revolutionaries, Feuilly earns his living as a fanmaker and is self-educated.

Mademoiselle Gillenormand

Monsieur Gillenormand's eldest daughter is a prudish, narrow-minded old woman who runs her father's household.

Monsieur Gillenormand

Monsieur Gillenormand, Marius Pontmercy's grandfather and caretaker, is a relic of the past. He had his heyday in the decadent Ancien Régime, the pre-Revolutionary monarchy, in which the nobility dominated France. He still looks back to those days with nostalgia and regret. Gillenormand believes that in modern times people lack the gift of living life to the fullest and enjoying all of its pleasures. He raises Marius to believe that the Revolution "was a load of scoundrels." When Marius discovers that his father was a Revolutionary hero, it causes a bitter break between them.

Théodule Gillenormand

Théodule is Monsieur Gillenormand's great-nephew and a lieutenant in the army. He is a vain young man and a favorite of his Aunt Gillenormand. He tries to become Gillenormand's favorite when Marius is out of the picture, but he can't replace Marius in the old man's affections.

Grantaire

Although Grantaire belongs to the ABC Society, he is a cynic and a hedonist and does not believe in the ideals of revolution. But he does believe in one ideal: Enjolras, whom he regards with love and admiration.

Inspector Javert

Inspector Javert is nearly as renowned a character as Jean Valjean, perhaps due to the dramatized versions of *Les Misérables,* which have tended to present the novel as more of a detective story than a morality tale. Javert serves as Valjean's nemesis throughout the novel, continually threatening to expose his past and bring him under the control of the law. In his exaggerated, nearly fanatical devotion to duty and his lack of compassion, Javert represents a punitive, vengeful form of justice.

Hugo suggests that Javert's "respect for authority and hatred of revolt" are rooted in his past, for he was born in a prison. As if to compensate for this fact, he has spent his life in faithful service to law enforcement. When Valjean saves Javert by helping him escape from the revolutionaries, Javert's rigid system of behavior is upset, for he realizes that Valjean, a criminal who has not yet been officially punished, has performed an act of great kindness and courage. Javert previously would have overlooked such an act and arrested the criminal, but his realization proves more than he can bear. Unable to resolve his inner conflict, Javert drowns himself in the Seine River.

Joly

A member of the ABC Society, Joly is studying medicine. He is something of a hypochondriac.

Monsieur Mabeuf

An elderly churchwarden, Mabeuf befriends Marius's father, Colonel Pontmercy, and Marius becomes friends with Mabeuf after his father dies. He is a gentle man whose main interests in life are his garden and his books, but he becomes very poor and has to sell all of his books. Impoverished and without hope in life, Mabeuf joins the rebels, courageously climbs to the top of the barricade to plant a flag, and is shot by the militia. His age and gentleness make his courage even more remarkable, showing that revolution can come in any form.

Madame Magloire

Madame Magloire is the personal maid of Mademoiselle Baptistine and the Bishop of Digne's housekeeper.

Charles Myriel

Myriel is a kind and generous bishop who gives Jean Valjean aid when everyone else refuses him. Searching for a place to spend the night, the exconvict finds that he is a branded man and no inn will let him stay. His last resort is the home of the bishop, who takes him in and treats him as an honored guest. After Valjean steals the Bishop's silver and is caught by the police, the bishop protects him by insisting that the silver was actually a gift. Afterward, he says to Valjean, "[You] no longer belong to what is evil but to what is good. I have bought your soul to save it from black thoughts and the spirit of perdition, and I give it to God." The bishop's selfless act inspires Valjean to change his life.

Colonel Georges Pontmercy

A hero of the Napoleonic wars, Pontmercy marries Gillenormand's youngest daughter and has a son, Marius. The villainous innkeeper, Thénardier, drags Pontmercy to safety from the battle-field of Waterloo. Although Marius does not meet his father, Pontmercy watches him from afar in church and loves his son. He leaves Marius a note telling him to adopt the title of Baron (Napoleon gave it to Pontmercy on the field of battle), and to do Thénardier every good in his power. Marius worships his father as a hero and is strongly influenced by his political beliefs.

Marius Pontmercy

Marius is a young law student who falls in love with Cosette. He also saves Valjean from a plot against his life by the innkeeper-turned-criminal, Thénardier. In turn, Marius is saved by Valjean while fighting on the barricade. He is the son of Georges Pontmercy, a colonel and war hero under Napoleon. But Marius's grandfather, Monsieur Gillenormand, despises Georges and takes Marius into his own home to raise him.

Marius is at a stage of life where he doesn't

know yet what he believes. His image of the world keeps opening up as he encounters new points of view. When Marius discovers his father's identity, he worships him as a war hero and adopts a pro-Napoleon stance opposed to his grandfather's royalism. He gets into a quarrel with Gillenormand and storms out of the house to make his way through Paris as a starving student. Marius falls in with a group of students, the ABC Society led by Enjolras, who share his republican beliefs. At first he is reluctant to give up his belief that conquest and war are the greatest ideals of a nation. But he begins to have doubts when the students present him with a new ideal, freedom: "Having so lately found a faith, must he renounce it? He told himself that he need not; he resolved not to doubt, and began despite himself to do so." When unrest stirs Paris in 1832 and his friends take up arms, he joins them on the barricades. But it is more out of desperation, because he fears he has lost Cosette, than out of political conviction. He is lured there by the voice of the street girl Eponine Thénardier telling him that his friends await him.

Jean Prouvaire

Prouvaire is a member of the ABC Society of students and workers. A wealthy student, he is interested in social questions, but is also a poet and lover with a romantic side.

Eponine Thénardier

The poor daughter of the Thénardiers, Eponine falls in love with Marius and becomes jealous of his love for Cosette. She is torn between wanting to help him and wanting to keep him away from Cosette. She courageously saves his life on the barricade by stepping between him and a bullet, and dies in his arms. Her life is an example of poverty's degradation: "What it came to was that in the heart of our society, as at present constituted, two unhappy mortals [Eponine and her sister] had been turned by extreme poverty into monsters at once depraved and innocent, drab creatures without name or age or sex, no longer capable of good or evil, deprived of all freedom, virtue, and responsibility; souls born yesterday and shrivelled today like flowers dropped in the street which lie fading in the mud until a cartwheel comes to crush them."

Gavroche Thénardier

Gavroche is a Parisian urchin (street child), the son of the villainous Thénardiers. Lively and clever, he lives by his wits. He dies by them as well and proves his courage, getting shot by soldiers when he teases them on the barricade. His fate is interwoven with that of Marius, Cosette, and the Thénardiers. The novel presents him as an essential representative of Paris: "He had neither hearth nor home, nor any regular source of food; yet he was happy because he was free. By the time the poor have grown to man's estate they have nearly always been caught in the wheels of the social order and become shaped to its requirements; but while they are children their smallness saves them."

Madame Thénardier

The coarse wife of the innkeeper Thénardier, she takes in Fantine's daughter, Cosette. But she treats her like a Cinderella, feeding and clothing her poorly and making her do the worst work in the household. She helps hatch a plot to entrap Valjean and steal his fortune, but instead ends up in prison. The narrator states that she is naturally cruel and scheming and offers her as an example of those who commit crimes not because they are driven to it, but because it suits them.

Monsieur Thénardier

The unscrupulous innkeeper and his wife take care of Cosette, but treat her poorly. He embarks on a life of crime, getting involved with the worst criminals in Paris, and attempts to entrap and rob Valjean. Although he ends up in prison, he escapes. He helps Valjean escape from the sewers when Valjean is trapped there with Marius. Thénardier plays a central part in the plot. He does good in spite of his evil intentions, not knowing what the consequences of his own actions will be.

Felix Tholomyés

A wealthy, rakish student, Tholomyés is Fantine's lover for a while and then abandons her. Their affair ruins Fantine. She becomes pregnant and cannot earn enough to save herself and her child. The narrator says of the relationship: "For him it was a passing affair, for her the love of her life."

Jean Vaijean

The chief protagonist, Jean Valjean, is an exconvict who struggles to redeem himself morally and to find acceptance in a society that rejects him as a former criminal. Valjean's redemption through his many trials is the central plot of *Les Misérables.*

The child of a poor peasant family, he loses both his parents as a young child and moves in with an older sister. When her husband dies, Valjean supports her and her seven children by working as a tree pruner. Unable to feed the family on his earnings, he steals a loaf of bread from a baker and ends up serving nineteen years in prison for his crime. Finally free, he finds that he cannot find lodging, work, or acceptance in the outside world. As an exconvict he is at the bottom of the social order.

But Valjean has a transforming experience when he meets the Bishop of Digne, who accepts and shelters him regardless of his past, even after Valjean tries to steal from his household. Here Valjean learns the lesson of unconditional love, a reason for living that sustains him through all of his trials. And they are many. He lives on the run from two forces: the justice of the law, represented by Javert, a police detective who doggedly pursues him, and his own conscience, which leads him to make difficult choices between what is right and what is easiest.

Valjean starts a new life as the mayor of Montreuil sur Mer. He is the savior of this manufacturing town, rebuilding its industries and economy and sustaining the population with new jobs. But he lives on the run from his dogged pursuer, Javert, and in his first moral trial he has to give himself up to keep an innocent man from going to prison in his place. He escapes again and lives the rest of his life as a fugitive.

The harshness of the society in which he lives presents great obstacles to Valjean's moral redemption. Only the transforming power of love lets him overcome them. He loves a young girl, Cosette, daughter of the prostitute Fantine, and raises her as his daughter. Most of his good acts center on her welfare: saving the life of her lover, Marius; protecting her, whatever the cost to himself; even giving up Cosette after she marries, so that she will not be sullied by connection to an exconvict. His love for her teaches him how to act in the world at large. In all of his actions he strives to be honorable and generous.

Change and Transformation

The most important theme the novel examines is that of transformation, in the individual and in society. Jean Valjean, the chief protagonist, is transformed from a misanthropic and potentially violent ex-convict to a man capable of heroic love and self-sacrifice. The force that transforms him is love. The Bishop of Digne offers Valjean unconditional love, trusting the former criminal with his life and giving him all that he can. Valjean finds inspiration for an entirely new life from this example. He learns to put another person first when he raises Cosette as his own daughter, and he endures moral trials, such as risking his life to rescue Marius, who loves Cosette and whom Valjean hates. On a broader scale, the workers and students on the barricade fight for social transformation, to create a new France without injustice and poverty.

Human Rights

Closely related to the theme of transformation is that of human rights. This is what the barricade is about and what the students, workers, and downtrodden poor of Paris want. The novel offers many examples of the violation of human rights. Valjean steals a loaf of bread because he has hungry children to feed. The law punishes him for nineteen years because of this petty crime, and Valjean finds little peace at the end of his term. The police inspector Javert pursues him almost to the grave for the theft of a coin. Fantine loves a man who abandons her, and she ends up as a prostitute. She sacrifices her child, her looks, and her body just to survive. Even worse, when she does defend her human dignity and accuses a bourgeois gentleman of assault, the police arrest her. As the novel presents it, the aim of revolution is to create a society in which all individuals have equal rights and in which poverty itself is undesirable.

Class Conflict

The central struggle is also a class conflict: revolution mobilizes the have-nots against the haves. The working class of Paris is presented as an ominous force, ready to throw up a barricade at a moment's notice. The barricade is where the life-and-death struggle of the disenfranchised and the government takes place. The students and workers join and fight to create a new and better nation, even at the cost of their lives. Enjolras, their leader, puts it eloquently when he says: " [This] is the hard price that must be paid for the future. A revolution is a toll-gate. But mankind will be liberated, uplifted and consoled. We here affirm it, on this barricade."

Justice and Injustice

Another major question the novel considers is

whether the legal institutions of the state exact true justice. While he is in prison, the convict Jean Valjean considers the question of whether he has been treated fairly. Readers must wonder if his crime, stealing a loaf of bread to feed his family, really merits the punishment he receives: four years of imprisonment that stretch to nineteen when he tries to escape. Valjean asks himself "whether human society had the right to ... grind a poor man between the millstones of need and excess—need of work and excess of punishment. Was it not monstrous that society should treat in this fashion precisely those least favored in the distribution of wealth...?" He comes to the conclusion that, although he did commit a reprehensible crime, the punishment is out of proportion, and he develops an intense hatred for society as a whole. Fantine meets the same fate when she defends herself against attack. As a prostitute, she is on the bottom rung of society; the law offers her no protection. Only respectable people with money appear to have any legal rights.

Meaning of Life

Valjean's great discovery, the one that transforms him, is that the meaning of life lies in love. His love is twofold, both the generalized love for one's fellow creatures that the Bishop of Digne shows toward him and the specific love for another person that he feels for Cosette. Summing up this philosophy at the end of his life, Valjean says to Cosette and Marius, "Love one another always.

There is nothing else that matters in this world except love."

Structure

In some ways the novel is structured traditionally. It has a rising action, that is, the part of the narrative that sets up the problems that are to be resolved. This consists of Valjean's life up to the point when he saves his enemy Marius by carrying him through the sewers of Paris to safety. The climax, or turning point, when the conflict reaches its peak, is the suicide of the police detective Javert. Caught between his rigid belief in the absolute power of law and his conclusion that he has a moral obligation to break the law and free his savior, Valjean, Javert solves his dilemma by killing himself. The denouement, or winding-down of the story, which describes the outcome of the primary plot problem as well as resolving secondary plots, includes Marius's recovery, the marriage of Cosette and Marius, the revelation of Valjean's true story, and the young couple's visit to Valjean's deathbed.

But the narrative's many departures from the main plot are important to the novel as well. The novel includes separate sections on the sewers of Paris, the criminal underworld, the convent, Parisian street slang, the Battle of Waterloo, revolutionary societies, and the barricades. Hugo is telling more than the story of one man; he is telling the story of Paris. His digressions, although they do not forward plot development, give the reader information about the novel's themes, such as human rights, justice and injustice, class conflict, and the city. He is primarily concerned not so much with narrating a story but with critiquing society and presenting his notions of reform.

Topics for Further Study

- Investigate current prison conditions in the United States and compare today's prison experience to Valjean's as described in the novel.

- Consider the ethical issues surrounding imprisonment that the novel raises in book two, chapter seven ("The inwardness of despair"). Does Hugo see prison as an effective means of punishing criminals? Does prison reform criminals, according to Hugo, or does it make them more violent? How does the author suggest prisoners should be treated? Use examples from the book to support your answers.

- Investigate the economic, legal, and social definition of poverty in the United States today and compare it to the conditions of poverty in Paris as described in the novel.

Point of View

The story is told from a third-person omniscient point of view. Omniscient narrators have a god's-eye or all-knowing view, knowing more than their characters do. The narrator breaks in several times to equate himself with the author. For example, at the beginning of the Waterloo episode, the narrator says: "On a fine May morning last year (that is to say, in the year 1861) a traveller, the author of this tale, walked from Nivelles in the direction of La Hulpe." And in describing Paris, he states: "For some years past the author of this book, who regrets the necessity to speak of himself, has been absent from Paris." Although generally there is a distinction between the author and the narrator of a work, this device blurs the boundary. The novel is a vehicle of expression for the author's social views. Whenever the narrator is not describing the actions, thoughts, and speech of the characters, the voice of authority emerges. This includes the discussion of

Parisian street urchins, the sewers, the underworld, and the barricades. The narrator pulls back from the characters to look at the broader scenario. Here is a typical example of this device, describing the barricade: "And while a battle that was still political was preparing in that place that had witnessed so many revolutionary acts; while the young people, the secret societies, and the schools, inspired by principle, and the middle-class inspired by self-interest, were advancing on each other to clash and grapple ... there was to be heard the sombre growling of the masses: a fearful and awe-inspiring voice in which were mingled the snarl of animals and the words of God, a terror to the fainthearted and a warning to the wise, coming at once from the depths, like the roaring of a lion, and from the depths like the voice of thunder."

Setting

The setting for most of the novel is Paris around 1830, a character in its own right. The narrative devotes almost as much space to it as to the protagonist, Valjean. It is a dark, gloomy, and sinister place, full of plague-carrying winds and polluting sewers, rotting old districts and slums. Its secretive aspect is a blessing, though, for Valjean, who seeks refuge in dark corners. The narrow alleys lend themselves, too, to the building of barricades. The narrative also presents Paris as a microcosm, reflecting the world as a whole: "Paris stands for the world. Paris is a sum total, the ceiling of the human race.... To observe Paris is to review the whole course of history...." Paris also has its places of beauty and tranquillity, such as the Luxembourg Garden on a fair day, but even here discontent lurks, in the form of two hungry boys wandering in search of food.

The novel presents Paris in all its wretchedness and grandeur. The urban environment has power over those who live in it. Some characters, such as Thénardier, an innkeeper who gets involved with the worst criminal elements of the city, are corrupted by Paris's temptations and hardships. Others, like Gavroche, the street urchin who is Th nardier's son, demonstrate courage and compassion in spite of their circumstances. For Valjean, Paris is both a refuge and a testing-ground. Hugo ranges over many aspects of the city in his portrayal of it, from the convents to the argot, or slang, spoken on the streets, from the heart of the city to its half-tamed outskirts, from rooftops to sewers. The sewer system of Paris symbolizes the dark underside of the city, where its secret history is stored: "that dreadful place which bears the impress of the revolution of the earth and of men, in which the remains of every cataclysm is to be found, from the Flood to the death of Marat." (Marat was a leader of the French Revolution who was assassinated.) Most of all, the citizens of Paris make up its character. The novel presents a sprawling picture of the people: criminals, orphans, students, the middle class, and others.

Symbolism

The novel employs symbolism, the use of one object to represent another, on a grand scale. Paris represents the world as a whole. Gavroche symbolizes the heroism of the average individual. The city sewers represent the seamy underside of Paris, filled with scraps of history, both good and evil, that have been discarded and forgotten, but not destroyed. The sewers also represent Valjean's passage through hell to redemption. He carries Marius to safety on his back through their passages like a martyr bearing a cross. A pair of silver candlesticks, stolen from the Bishop, serves for Valjean as a symbolic reminder of where he has come from and how he should act. Such leitmotivs, or recurring themes, woven through the text add depth and meaning.

Romanticism

Romanticism was an artistic and intellectual movement of the late eighteenth and early nineteenth century that put the individual mind at the center of the world and of art. Romanticism valued emotional and imaginative responses to reality, the individual's interior experience of the world, which it perceived as being closer to truth. It evolved partly as a reaction to the Enlightenment's emphasis on restraint, simplicity, logic, and respect for tradition. *Les Misérables* is a characteristic Romantic work in both theme and form. In theme, the novel assaults the traditional social structure, glorifies freedom of thought and spirit, and makes a hero of the average individual, such as Gavroche the street urchin, who dies with courage on the barricade. In form, the novel values content over structure, offers passionate rhetoric rather than classical restraint, and ranges freely over many subjects.

Romanticism

Romanticism was an intellectual and artistic movement that swept Europe and the United States in the late-eighteenth to mid-nineteenth centuries. This movement was preceded by the Enlightenment, which emphasized reason as the basis of social life. The Enlightenment also promoted universal, formal standards, dating back to Greek and Roman classicism, for greatness in art. The artists, philosophers, writers, and composers of the Romantic movement rejected these standards and instead valued the individual imagination and experience as the basis of art and source of truth. Nature, the state of childhood, and emotion, rather than logic or scientific investigation, were considered the primary sources of eternal truth.

Victor Hugo was one of the leading writers of the Romantic movement in France, and *Les Misérables* was one of its major works. The novel is Romantic in style and theme. It is written in a sweeping, emotional manner, taking the experience of the individual as the starting-point for discovering truths about French society.

Compare & Contrast

- **1830s:** Under public pressure,

French legislators reformed prisons to some extent. They abolished some of the more barbaric forms of punishment that were practiced under the *Ancien Régime,* such as torture and hanging, and offered education for petty offenders.

1850s: As a result of unemployment caused by industrialization, crime rates rose in France and the prison population increased. Inmates were not allowed to speak to each other. Riots and suicides took place in prisons.

Today: Due in part to poor economic conditions in France, prison populations are on the rise again, with an increase in the number of convicts serving time for drug-related crimes. With a prison population that is steadily increasing, overcrowding is a problem, and many inmates find themselves sharing a cell with as many as five other prisoners.

- **1830s:** France was beginning to become an industrialized nation, a process that would transform its economy, workplace, working class, and political landscape.

   1850s: Increasing industrialization brought wealth to France as well as increased unemployment. Lack of work drove thousands of poor women to prostitution and many of the urban poor to crime.

Today: After rapid consolidation of industries in the 1970s, many French manufacturing jobs were eliminated, resulting in high levels of unemployment. Currently, many young people have difficulty finding permanent work. However, recent changes in the French school system have expanded educational opportunities for students, in an effort by the government to create an employable workforce.

- **1830s:** Antigovernment protesters set up barricades in Paris after Charles X published three ordinances calling to abolish freedom of the press, dissolve Parliament, and limit voting rights to 25,000 landed proprietors. The 1830 revolution successfully removed Charles from the throne; succeeding him was Louis Phillippe.

  1850s: A bloody protest occurred in Paris in 1848, removing Louis Phillippe from power and creating a provisional government that extended the right to vote and set up national workshops to combat unemployment. After another violent clash, this government was in turn replaced by the Second Republic, with an assembly dominated by the middle class.

Today: After violent student protests and nation-wide strikes in May of 1968, new French leaders shifted toward a more liberal form of government, trying to balance a market economy while preserving social-democratic principles. Today, France is joining with other European nations to create the European Union, a community which will share a common currency and create a formidable trading bloc.

Revolution

France in the nineteenth century was in a constant state of political and social unrest. In 1789, the newly formed National Assembly created a document called the "Declaration of the Rights of Man," establishing the right to liberty, equality, property, and security, and adding that every citizen had a duty to defend these rights. After King Louis XVI was executed on January 21, 1793, a period of confusion and violence followed. Many people, the innocent along with the guilty, were executed in the aftermath of the Revolution.

With the bloody departure of the monarchy, the legislature appointed a five-man Directory to power in 1795. But conspirators, including Napoleon Bonaparte, staged a coup d'état, or surprise overthrow of the state, in 1799. Napoleon became dictator and remained in power until he was completely defeated at the Battle of Waterloo in 1815. This is when Hugo's novel *Les Misérables* begins.

From 1815 until 1830, France was ruled by Louis XVIII and then Charles X under the Second Restoration. During this time the French used a constitutional monarchy where the king governed alongside an elected parliament. This was a comparatively tranquil and prosperous period, but it ended in the Revolution of 1830, when Charles X published ordinances dissolving Parliament, limiting voting rights to land owners, and abolishing freedom of the press. Charles was forced from the throne and replaced by Louis Philippe, the "citizen king," who had fought in the French Revolution. This was a triumph for the middle class, but it left the working-class and poor out in the cold.

The insurrection of 1832, the first Republican uprising since 1789, started to stir at the burial of Lamarque, a Revolutionary hero. Republicans shouted, "Down with Louis Philippe!" The barricades went up, and a violent clash ensued. The forces on the barricades, composed mainly of students and workers, lacked public support, and the rebellion was put down by government forces.

In 1848, a new wave of revolution swept across Europe, triggered by the political unrest of bourgeois liberals and nationalists, crop failures several years in a row, and economic troubles. In France, Louis Philippe was driven from his throne. After a bloody struggle between the working-class and the middle-class provisional government in Paris, the Second Republic was established, with a mainly middle-class national assembly and Louis Napoleon, who was related to Napoleon I, as president.

Hugo was sympathetic to the 1848 revolution, became a representative in the assembly, and initially supported Louis Napoleon. However, in 1851 the president assumed control of France in a military coup d'état, and in 1852 the population voted to disband the republic and reestablish the empire. Hugo was disillusioned with both the French people who were willing to exchange freedom for stability and with Napoleon III, who had traded in his republican opinions to become a dictator. Criticizing the government and Louis Napoleon publicly, Hugo was forced to leave France, first for Belgium and then for the Channel Islands. *Les Misérables,* which Hugo composed from the late 1840s to 1862 during his exile, integrated his feelings about the political situation, his memories of the barricades of 1848, and his republican ideals. The novel denounces the degradation of the urban working-class and society's mistreatment and neglect of the poor, especially women and children.

Industrialization

The continuing industrialization of France in the 1850s and 1860s created wealth for the country, but it also created unemployment as machines replaced manual laborers in many jobs. This in turn led to an increase in crime. Poor working women turned to prostitution as a means of survival, working under the scrutiny of a Police Morals Bureau, which considered them corrupt. The character of Jean Valjean was drawn from a historical person, a petty thief named Pierre Maurin who spent five years in prison for stealing bread for his sister's children. Hugo draws a clear distinction in the novel between those who choose crime because they are corrupt and those who are driven to it by poverty and desperation. On the one hand, there is Thénardier, who is by nature "highly susceptible to the encroachments of evil." On the other, there is Valjean, who stole only to save his family, and Fantine, who suffered for protecting her own child. The narrator blames society's indifference and injustice for the situation of those who fall into the latter category.

Critical Overview

Publishers bid against each other for the right to publish *Les Misérables,* no doubt sensing that the novel would be a great success. It had been awaited for years. The author's exile to Guernsey only increased his international reputation and the suspense of waiting for his next major work. Hugo received an unheard-of 300,000 francs as advance payment for the novel. But the publishers regained their investment and more when the book came out.

Les Misérables appeared in 1862, published by LaCroix of Brussels and Paris. It appeared simultaneously in Paris, London, Brussels, New York, Berlin, St. Petersburg, and other European capitals. Published initially in five parts, divided into ten volumes, the novel was released in three separate installments in April, May, and June. Hugo's family and friends gave it a huge buildup in the press, advertising its release for a month in advance in all the major papers of Europe. Rumors that it might be banned in France built up the suspense even more. The book-buying public gave it an enthusiastic reception. Booksellers in Paris lined up to buy the second installment in such great numbers that police were needed to manage the crowd. It was an enormous success for its publishers and its author. Adèle Hugo, the author's wife, wrote that groups of workers shared the cost of the ten volumes in order to pass it from hand to hand and read it. The critic Saint-Beuve commented that

Hugo "had snatched the greatest popularity of our time under the nose of the very government that exiled him. His books go everywhere: the women, the common people, all read him. Editions go out of print between eight in the morning and noon."

The book's critical reception, on the other hand, was mixed. Some of his contemporaries perceived Hugo's style as long-winded, digressive, melodramatic, and full of unlikely coincidences. Others found his sweeping, passionate prose, championing of social issues, and ideals of justice and morality inspirational.

On the negative side, many critics disliked the novel's digressions from the main plot, especially the long account of Waterloo. Adolphe Thiers, a historian, expressed the strong opinion that the novel was "detestable. The spirit is bad, the plan is bad, and the execution is bad." The writer Barbey D'Aurévilly found the novel vulgar and full of improbabilities, and criticized it for its socialist views. Hippolyte Taine, a critic and historian, thought the novel was insincere and its success was a flash in the pan.

On the positive side, the poet Charles Baudelaire offered praise for the work's poetic and symbolic qualities. The English novelist George Meredith, though he thought it was drawn in over-simplified terms, called it "the masterwork of fiction of this century—as yet. There are things in it quite wonderful." The great Russian novelist Fyodor Dostoevsky considered *Les Misérables* superior to his own *Crime and Punishment,* and saw Hugo as a champion of the idea of spiritual rebirth. Walter Pater was of the opinion that Hugo's works were among the finest products of the Romantic movement.

In the first half of the twentieth century, Hugo's reputation as a novelist waned. This was in part because of changes in the tastes of writers and readers. First the Realist, then the Modernist writers swept through the literary scene, and it is characteristic of such movements that they debunk what has come before in an effort to break new ground. *Les Misérables* in particular achieved its blinding success partly because of the moment in time when it was released. It was the long-awaited work of a national hero returning from exile, but that historical moment passed, along with Hugo's great influence over national opinion.

But many writers, including André Gide and Jean-Paul Sartre, acknowledged his lasting influence. Hugo's works are still widely read today, and he has modem defenders. The literary critic Victor Brombert, for example, comments: "The dramatic and psychological power of Hugo's novels depends in large part on the creation of archetypal figures.... The sweep of his texts and the moving, even haunting images they project are a function of the widest range of rhetorical virtuosity." *Les Misérables* has passed into modern legend in its well-known and popular adaptations for film and the stage, and it is arguably the most important Romantic novel of the nineteenth century.

Sources

Victor Brombert, *Victor Hugo and the Visionary Novel,* Harvard University Press, 1984.

Matthew Josephson, *Victor Hugo: A Realistic Biography of the Great Romantic,* Doubleday, 1942.

Joanna Richardson, *Victor Hugo,* St. Martin's Press, 1976.

For Further Study

Elliot Grant, *The Career of Victor Hugo,* Harvard University Press, 1945.

> A very basic and useful study of Hugo's main novels and poetry.

Richard B. Grant, *The Perilous Quest: Image, Myth, and Prophecy in the Narration of Victor Hugo,* Duke University Press, 1968.

> Hugo described himself as a "prophef" among men, as a translator of myths. This book analyzes this theme by examining Hugo's major novels.

Kathryn M. Grossman, *Les Misérables: Conversion, Revolution, Redemption,* Twayne, 1996.

> Aimed specifically toward students, this work praises the novel as a book that "enables us to escape into the adventures of others: it brings us back to ourselves."

John Porter Houston, *Victor Hugo,* Twayne, 1988.

> A good introduction to Hugo's life and works.

Patricia Ward, *The Medievalism of Victor Hugo,* Pennsylvania State University Press, 1975.

> Hugo was fascinated by the

mysteries and secrets of medieval times. Although *Les Misérables* cannot really be called a Gothic novel, some of its episodes, like those in the sewers, belong to the genre.

CPSIA information can be obtained
at www.ICGtesting.com
Printed in the USA
BVHW040854090420
577228BV00013B/340